Akampurira Abraham

Development economics

An aspect of development

Anchor Academic
Publishing

Abraham, Akampurira: Development economics. An aspect of development, Hamburg, Anchor Academic Publishing 2013

Buch-ISBN: 978-3-95489-164-1
PDF-eBook-ISBN: 978-3-95489-664-6
Druck/Herstellung: Anchor Academic Publishing, Hamburg, 2013

Bibliografische Information der Deutschen Nationalbibliothek:
Die Deutsche Nationalbibliothek verzeichnet diese Publikation in der Deutschen Nationalbibliografie; detaillierte bibliografische Daten sind im Internet über http://dnb.d-nb.de abrufbar.

Hermannstal 119k, 22119 Hamburg
http://www.diplomica-verlag.de, Hamburg 2013
Printed in Germany

Table of Contents

CHAPTER ONE

ECONOMIC GROWTH AND DEVELOPMENT

1. Introduction

Development economics entail all the aspects of the development process especially meant for the developing countries to overcome the challenges that impede development. This can be through education, education and man power development, restructuring market incentives, incorporating favorable social and political approaches and practices among other factors.

Human beings however need streamlined social and economic systems that are able to achieve development through major changes in social structures, national institutions, cultures and attitudes as well as eradication of poverty, reduction of income inequality and acceleration of economic growth. The developing world needs a multi disciplinary approach and ideas so as to come out of the economic backward situation. Micheal, P. (2003: 9) describes that because of heterogeneity of the developing world, and the complexity of the development process, development economics must be eclectic, attempting to combine relevant concepts and theories from traditional economics analysis along with new models and broader multi disciplinary approaches from historical and co temporally development experience of Africa, Asia, and Latin America. Debraj Ray (2007) puts it that development economics studies economics of the developing world and has made excellent use of economic theory, econometrics, anthropology, sociology, political science, biology and demography. It needs a lot more dimensional approach to understand it. Other scholars have tried to bring about the key issues that are in development economics such as Dasgupta (1998), Hoff, Braverman and stiglitz (1993), Ray (1998), Bardhan and Udry (1999), Mookerjee and Ray (2001), and Sen(1999).

1.1. Definition

Economic growth refers to a rise in national income or per capita income. If the production of goods in a nation rises by whatever means one can speak of that rise as economic growth. Maunder (1996 : 462) asserts that potential growth is largely determined by the factors of production a nation has and also how these factors are effectively combined and developed.

On the other hand economic development includes not merely economic growth but steady progress towards absolute poverty elimination. A sustained increase in employment and a reduction of inequality contribute to economic development.

Some economists take development as purely an economic phenomenon in which rapid gains from overall growth of GNP and income per capita would automatically bring benefits "trickle down" to the masses in form of jobs and other economic opportunities. Time has also shown that without adequate economic growth, economic development cannot be sustained in the long run. But economic growth and development need not be the same.

1.2. Differences between growth and development

1. Using quality of life regarded as an important index of development is contended that such quality is not adequately reflected in the index of a country X may have a lower per capita real income than the other income but the quality of life enjoyed by citizens of X may be better than of Y. several factors are used in measurement of such quality such as education and literacy rates, life expectancy, the level of nutrition, consumption of energy per head, consumption of consumer durables per head.
2. Another source of difference between growth and development place is the question of externality and non marketability. The GNP captures only those means of wellbeing that happen to be transacted in the market and leaves out benefits and costs that do not have a price tag attached to them. The importance of what is left out has become increasingly recognized as awareness of the contribution of the environment and natural resources to our well being has grown. Economies have externalities for example in physical and human capital as noted by Romer (1986), Lucas (1988), Azariadis and Drazen (1990). There is thus low average income to society, high inequality and high poverty rates.
3. Economic growth is usually only concerned with GNP per head and does not take into account the distribution of that GNP among the population. It is of course possible for a country to have an expansion of GNP per head while its distribution becomes more unequal possibly even with the poorest groups going down absolutely in terms of their real incomes. For instance in Uganda (1945- 1960) a period of rising incomes brought about largely by favorable prices of primary products as benefits were both more immediate and more widespread because they accrued to most of the cultivators of small farms in central part of the country. But areas further

away from the railway still did not pay to grow crops for export and consequently inequality in Uganda came to take the form of growing regional disparity of income. Even when the markets do exist, the valuation of commodities in GNP will reflect the biases that markets may have. There are important problems in dealing with different prices in different parts of the world. Even for a given economy, the relative importance that is attached to one commodity compared to with other may be distorted visa- vis what might be achieved under perfectly competitive conditions if the market operations happens to be institutionally imperfect or if equilibrium outcomes do not prevail. Keneth J. Arrow (2011: 493), emphasizes on the traditional explanations of unemployment focus on market rigidities which ignores the characteristics in the product market. What takes place in the product market influences unemployment and economic growth.

4. The real incomes enjoyed by a person in a given year reflects at best the extent of the wellbeing enjoyed by that person at that particular period of time. However in assessing what kind of life the person has experienced in life we have to take a more integral view of that person's life. The issues to be considered include interdependence over time as well as the elementary question of life. GNP information does not adequately capture the details of what goes on period by period within the society welfare therefore GNP remains fundamentally inadequate for the concept of development.
5. It must be noted that GNP is a measure of the amount of a means of a wellbeing that people have and it does not tell us how the people are involved in succeeding to getting out of these means given their ends.

   It is possible that while per capita income is increasing, per capita consumption may also be falling.

   If the on the whole an increase in output is devoted to building up of a country's military strength or putting monumental buildings, with which to impress the population and foreign visitors it may not impact on development. The assessment of economic development therefore has to go beyond GNP information.

   Another aspect of GNP is where there may be increasing incomes accompanied by a widening income inequality. Income inequality is believed to have an impact on economic growth. Barro (2000) inequality is negatively associated with growth in poor countries, and positively in rich countries. It negatively affects demand, human capital development and investment.

CHAPTER TWO

MEASUREMENT OF ECONOMIC DEVELOPMENT

2. Introduction

The most common way to assess and determine development is by reference to a country's GNP. GNP is a measure of its total output valued at the prices at which it is sold. International comparisons of GNP per head provide rough guidelines of relative welfare between countries or in the countries over time. The first difficulty is that national products of different countries are expressed in different currencies having different purchasing power both in international trade and at home.

Since they are expressed in a common currency, this has usually involved a conversion and official rate of exchange but at best these exchange rates reflect only the price relations of goods entering into international trade. In practice they frequently diverge substantially even from this since currencies are often overvalued or undervalued. A further problem arises in that foreign exchange rates cannot be used to measure the relative prices of goods and services that do not enter international trade (non trade goods). With that regard such goods and services, a currency may have a totally different purchasing power from that it may have over foreign goods.

Finally it is also arguable that the national products especially of very similar countries are made up of totally different goods and services and satisfy equally different needs determined by different climatic conditions and institutional factors such as the income of a Ugandan sustains him in Uganda but converted in dollars it may not provide him with enough food, shelter and clothes in America. On the other hand, the suggestion that Ugandans have less need for heating and therefore do not need so large an income to meet some of the harsh conditions of nature can be misinterpreted to having a better life in these areas. With the dissatisfaction of GNP as an economic development measure, certain economists try to measure it in terms of social indicators and these include health, food and nutrition, education including literacy and skills, employment, conditions of work, consumption of basic necessities, transportation, and housing including household facilities, clothing, recreation and entertainment, social security among other parameters.

2.1. Physical Quantity of Life Index (PQLI).

A policy is used only in three items i.e infant mortality, life expectancy and illiteracy rate in constructing PQLI relating to the 23 developed and developing countries of the World on the comparative study.

$$PQLI = f(im, e, L)$$
$$= (imI, ei, Li)/3$$

$$= 0.33imI + 0.33ei + 0.33Li$$

Where, e is life expectancy,

I is illiteracy,

Im is infant mortality.

Limitations of PQLI

1. There is a problem of assigning weights to various items which may depend upon the social economic and political set up of a country. This involves subjectivity. Scholars assign equal weight to the three indicators which undermines the value of the index in and comparison would be as inaccurate as GNP figures.
2. The majority of the indicators are inputs and not outputs such as education, health etc.

2.2. Human Development Index.

This is the most recent attempt to provide an aggregate measure of development and is now annually published by UNDP since 1990. It is an index of measuring national social economic development based on measure of life expectancy at birth, educational attainments and adjusted real per capita income.

Like PQLI, the HDI attempts to rank all countries at a scale of 0 (the lowest human index). Based on three goals or end products of development.

1. Longevity; Is measured by life expectancy at birth.
2. Knowledge; Is measured by a weighted average of adult illiteracy (2/3) and many years of schooling (1/3 weight).

3. Incomes as measured by adjusted real per capita income (adjusted for the dif fering purchasing power and for the assumption of rapidly diminishing mar ginal utility of income.

The three parameters mentioned are part of the core values of development outlined by Brinley Thomas (1954), i.e sustenance, self esteem, and freedom that represent common goals cherished by all individuals and societies.
In the HDI, proposed by UNDP,

$$HDI = g(Y, L, e)$$

Where, Y is adjusted real / per capita income,

e, is life expectancy,
L is literacy rate.

The index varies between 0 and 1. The index nearer to 1 the higher the level of human development. The human development has two components.

a) The actual achievement.
b) Shortfalls from a target or measure of deprivation.

An index which emphasizes the magnitude has tasks that lie ahead. The construction of the index of deprivation indicator is as follows;

$$DIYi = (\text{Max } Y - Yi)/(\text{Max } Y - \text{Min } Y).$$

It is important to note that many studies such as Strauss and Thomas (1995) show that human capital investment is correlated with family income. Carvalho (2000) put it that an increase in pension income resulted into a decrease in child labor and increase in school enrolment. The level of incomes greatly affects the other parameters such as life expectancy and human capital investment.

Limitations of HDI

1. One must always remember that the index is one of relative rather than absolute development so that all countries improve at the same weighted rate. The poorest countries will not get credit for their progress.
2. The national HDI may have unfortunate effect of shifting the focus away from the substantial inequality within countries.
3. The three indicators used are good but not ideal. For example the UN team wanted to use nutritional status of children under 5 years as the ideal health indicator but the data was not available.

   Some good work has been done to determine the relationship and dynamic interplay between growth and social institutions such as (Cole, Mailath and Postelwaithe (1992), (1998), (2001).). Well built up social institutions have a big bearing on the good well being of the people. In situations where poor institutions appear there is lack of proper governance, transparency and poor service delivery. Many studies stress that there is a strong association between aggregate investment and measures of bad institutions or corruption (e.g. Knack and Koefer (1995), Mauro (1995), and Svensson (1998)). Strong institutions are required for an increased investment, a pre-requisite to economic growth.
4. Its creation in part motivated by a political strategy designed to focus attention on health and education aspects of development.

CHAPTER THREE

POPULATION GROWTH AND DEVELOPMENT

3. Introduction

No agreed position has been reached on the effects of rapid population growth of developing countries on their economic growth. The assumption is that rapid population growth was detrimental as prevailed in 1950's and 1960's when the emphasis in the general development literature was on lack of capital coupled with surplus labor in agriculture as a major constraint in economic development. By late 1970's with attention shifting to efficiency with which capital and other factors of production were utilized and to the roles of policy in creating or distorting positive incentives of efficiency. Challenges arose to the conventional view that the apparent abundance of labor in poor countries compared to labor and land was hindering economic growth.

The following discussion is according to the points of view of analysis of macroeconomic consequences of rapid population growth. i.e the pessimists and optimists.

Malthus as a successor pessimist gave a simple model where he incorporates the classical ways theory that the supply of labor was completely elastic at subsistence level. In good times i.e when Average Product rose above the subsistence level, marriage occurred more often and earlier and couples had more children thus higher income per capita led to an increase in population and the supply of labor.

A population increase however eventually brought about falling wages and rising food prices as an increasing supply of labor run up against the fixity of land and given the diminishing returns, labor productivity fell with falling consumption, marriage, and fertility rates fell and mortality rates rose completing the cycle.

As a description of trends of several centuries preceding this 1801 essay, Malthus was likely to collect. Data put together by demographers and economic historians on wages, rents, food prices and fertility and mortality in England from the 14th century portions in the Malthus model.

As a predictor of the future, Malthus seemed to be wrong both about diminishing returns and about human productive behavior but by 19th century couples were practicing cautious control fertility within marriages leading to a smaller family size.

Malthus and the classical economists were writing at a time when in England population growth were accelerating with a new burst of population growth in developing countries after 2nd World war economists returned to Malthus tradition.

The analytical models Leibenstein (1954) and Nelson (1956) they introduced population as an endogenous variable influenced by income. In these models small increases in income at the subsistence level lead to increases in labor supply that swarm small houses in capital or other small displacement or stimuli to the economy. The result is a low level equilibrium trap.
Only massive capital formation or major stimulus can overcome the trap.
Early one sector neo classical model by Solow (1956) were similarly Malthusian in that the fast the rate of population growth and thus the more activity the increase in labor supply compared with capital formation, the lower the level of per capita income consumption. With the constant returns to scale and constant rate of saving the faster than the growth rate of labor force reduces the capital- labor ratio and the productivity of labor. More resources must be used to increase capital per head preventing immediate higher consumption in future period. Thus rapid population is harmful even in absence of diminishing returns. Population in these neoclassical state models, labor was treated as exogenous with no effort to incorporate the determination of population growth via the effects of economic change on mortality and fertility.
Population growth is also treated as exogenous and stimulates a negative effect in 2 sector growth models.

3.1. Optmists view

The pessimists' models have not gone unchallenged. Optimists view of population growth have tended to emphasize the critical contributors to economic growth. Such factors such as innovation, efficiency in the use of factors, human as opposed to physical capital and technological change in contrast to the neoclassical emphasis on the critical role of physical capital formation.

Optimists argue that a growing population is a net contributor of economic growth for 2 principle reasons.

a) Because of a large population brings economies of large scale of population and consumption.
b) Because population pressure and the scale economies. Population growth are likely to encourage technological innovations and organizational and institutional change particularly in agriculture.

In addition optimists argue that a growing population can stimulate demand and thus reduce investment risk and permits constant improvement of the labor force with better trained workers.

In a classical period Adam Smith involved scale and resultant induced innovation not only to explain economic growth itself but also as arguments for a positive effect of population growth on economic growth. He noted that growing population by widening the market and fostering creativity and innovation facilities and division of labor leading to higher productivity.

Later Marshal also emphasized economies of scale and innovation; noting that while the part which nature plays in production shows a tendency to diminishing returns, a part which man plays shows a tendency to increasing returns. Economies arise out of increased knowledge, greater specialization, better communication and organization changes all associated with increasing scale of production which might result from population growth.

In a modern era Kuznets and Hirschman and others have also emphasized the potential contribution of a growing population, scale economies and to innovation. But there has been limited effort to test the expected effects empirically and that effort has focused solely on the scale effect.

Glover and Simon report that a strongly positive elasticity of roads per unit area with respect to population density in a cross national analysis.

The most effective argument that population may encourage innovation has been made by Boserup (1981) for the agricultural sector. She suggests that increasing population densities induces a shift to a more labor intensive farming system. A shift from a long fallow to a more frequent cropping confronts farmers with a new innovation possibilities. A shift initially requires greater labor input which results in diminishing returns to labor. It will not occur unless rising population pressure necessitates it. Once such shifts occur the use of new tools and techniques permits large increases in productivity. On the other hand there are only historical but also co temporally examples that appear to refute Boserup argument. There are cases in the 19th century like China, Bangladesh and parts of Africa in the last 2 decades in which population growth has probably contributed to declining returns. Outside agriculture it is difficult to show that population pressure rather than other factors has been a major impediment to innovation.

The arguments of the optimists with the possible exception of the advantages of greater population density in rural areas though appealing are as poorly supported empirically and are difficult to support as arguments of the pessimists. The arguments rest largely on theory. The effects of population vary with time, place and circumstances must be studied empirically.

3.2. Fer and Ranis (1964) and Denis (1954)

In these 2 models surplus labor in agricultural sector is absorbed in the manufacturing economy. Savings and thus capital grow faster than population and technological change in dynamic manufacturing sector offsets the combining effects of research and development in agriculture and population growth.

All other things the same, the transfer of labor in main sector occurs more rapidly and the share of labor in manufacturing thus grow more rapidly the slower the growth of the population. Slower population growth thus speeds up the elimination of dualism that is a hindrance to economic growth.

These early growth models treated population growth and labor force growth as equivalent and ignored age structure. In these overlapping generation model Samuelson (1968) introduced a crude approximation of the age structure. He pointed out 2 age groups. A younger working population and older retired population. Younger generation transfers consumption (loans) to the older generation. The loans to be repaid by the subsequent generation of young workers. A sustained increase in population growth raises the population of the young group causing higher consumption transfers to the old. If a higher population growth rate persists, each generation benefits; thus Samuelson came to the opposite conclusion from that reached in neo classical growth a sustained higher population rate leads to higher life time economic welfare.

Samuelson ignored dependent children in effect assuming they cause no cost to the parents nor to the economy external to the household. In fact higher population growth that results from higher fertility will increase the proportion of children in a population and not increase labor supply for about 15 years. To the extent children consume more than they produce. Their existence must reduce the consumption or saving of workers or retirees.

In the tradition wholly different from the above analytic and deductive models Coale and Hoover (1958) developed a model highlighting the fact that children are costly and that higher fertility increases the proportion of children in the population. They built into their stimulation model of the economics of India the assumption that savings/ capital and thus investment /capital fall in proportion of non working dependants as the economy rises.

Using the model they made the protection of the per capita of India under low, high and fertility assumptions and concluded that over 30 year period per capita income could be as much as 40% high compared with low fertility assumption.

CHAPTER FOUR

PHYSICAL CAPITAL ACCUMULATION AND ECONOMIC DEVELOPMENT

4.1. Harrod -Domar Model

The simplest and best known production function are used in the analysis of economic development was developed independently in the period 1930's by economists Harrod and Domar. Primarily they explain the relationship between growth and unemployment in advanced capitalistic countries. But Harrod – Domar model has been used extensively in developing countries as a simple way of looking at the relationship between growth and capital requirements.

The underlying assumption of the model is that the output of any economic unit whether a firm, an industry or the whole economy depends on the amount of capital invested in that unit.

Thus if we call the output Y , and the stock of capital K, then Output Y can be related to Capital stock K.

$\Delta Y = \Delta K/k$

Where k is constant,

To convert this in the statement about the growth of output we use the notation Δ to represent increases in output Y and capital K.

$\Delta Y= \Delta K/k$

As the growth rate of output is simply incremental in output divided by the total amount of output i.e. $g = \Delta Y/Y$, where g is the growth rate.

Dividing both sides of the equation by Y,

$\Delta Y/Y =\Delta K/k.Y$

$g = \Delta K/Y. 1/k$

For the whole economy Δ is in K is the same as investment

$\Delta K = I =S$ hence

$\Delta K/Y$ becomes $I/Y = S/Y = s$

Equation (iii) becomes $g = s/k$

Which is a basic Harrod – Domar relationship for an economy.

Underlying this equation is the view that capital created by investment in plant and by equipment is the main determinant of growth and it is savings by people and corporations that make this investment possible.

The capital output ratio is simply a measure of productivity of capital or investment.
Economists often use the term incremental capital output ratio (ICOR) because in studying growth one is mainly interested in output of additional or incremental capital. The Incremental Capital Output Ratio refers to the relationship between the national stock of capital and its total national product.

Country	**ICOR**
Kenya	5.1
Tanzania	10.1
Brazil	4.8
USA.	5.6
Ivory Coast.	8.2
South Korea.	4.0
Japan.	5.1

4.2. Growth accounting Model.

The simple Harrod- Domar model $g = s/k$ production function obscures some of the basic differences in growth performance between nations. One wants to know much about why the capital output ratio varies so much. To that end economists such as Robert Solow and Edward Benson have attempted to explain the sources of growth with a different form of production function; one that allows the analyst to separate out the various causes of growth.

The production function used in this analysis includes more factors of production. The function relates increases in output to increases in inputs or capital, skilled and unskilled labor and other variables. This method also attempts to separate out the contribution made by rises in the efficiency with which inputs are used.

A production function take the following $Y = f(K, L, R, A)$

Where Y = output

K = stock of capital.

L = size of labor force.

R = stock of arable land.

A = increases in productivity/ efficiency with which inputs are used.

The next step is to convert this production function into a form that makes measuring the contribution of each input possible. The derivation of this new form of equation involves calculus and is represented in this form.

$G_Y = a + W_K \cdot g_k + W_L \cdot g_L + W_R + g_R$

g is the rate of growth of any variable.

W is the share of output of any input.

Y is the national output.

K is the capital.

R is the arable land/ natural resources.

A simple numerical example illustrates the way in which this equation is used.

Assume the following values of variable in the equation.

$g_Y = 0.06$ or growth rate of 6% per annum.

$g_K = 0.07$ or capital stock rises at 7% a year.

$g_L = 0.02$ or labor force increases at 2% a year.

$g_R = 0.01$ i.e. rising arable land by 1% a year.

Share of labour in national income is 0.6, share of capital is 0.3 and share of land is 10%

$a = 0.026$

This shows a productivity growth is 2.6% a year and thus accounts or just under a half the total growth of GNP of 6% a year.

The conclusions that have arisen from empirical work are as follows:

1. The available sources of growth calculations suggest that the impact of capital formation on growth is considerable in both developing and developed countries. At the early stages of development capital formation contribution to GDP is considerable whereas at higher levels of output productivity growth appears much more important. Studies in the middle income nations such as Korea, Philippines and Mexico indicate that in the 60's and 70's growth in the physical capital stock may have contributed from 1/3 of the output growth. The contribution is as much as ½ in poor countries.
2. Some of the increases in production efficiency or productivity involves advances in technology that are embodied in capital equipment.

In some areas especially the developing world, resources are not properly invested to boost capital accumulation. There are cases of funding unproductive ventures such as wars and other related conflicts. The channeling of resources to ongoing conflict will inhibit the accumulation of productive resources (Benhabib and Rustichini (1996), González (2007).

It is important to note that it is difficult to stimulate the desired level of domestic savings. This requires countries to have well institutions to mobilize domestic savings. Studies done such as (DFID, 2004), Zolt and Wang (1997), Hadjimichael et al (1994) have established the role of financial sector development and economic growth.

Harrod Domar's Warranted growth concept

Harrod begins his analysis by introducing the concept of the warranted rate of growth. This is the rate of growth which is determined by the values of the two crucial variables i.e. the planned natural rate of savings and the average value of capital output rates as planned by producers. Planned savings represents the sample of the savings power which individuals/

firm plans to withhold for consumption in the future period. The capital output ratio represents the value of capital needed to produce a given output divided by the value of that output; if planned savings are represented as a proportion of national income.
Then this proportion is divided by the planned capital- output ratio gives the warranted rate of growth of output.

$$G_W = S/C_P$$

For most of his analysis Harrod assumes that savings planned as a proportion of national income are fulfilled. He then focuses on planned capital output ratio. i.e. its determinants and consequences of failure by producers to achieve planned capital output ratio.

Harrod observes that planned capital output ratio is essentially technically determined. It represents the value of capital required to produce one unit of output in a given period of time.

In Harrod model output plans may not be fulfilled because aggregate demand may not be held as expected. Producers adjust immediately to unanticipated changes in demand. At first they may do so by working their plans over time in the case of demand increase or by accumulating unsold stocks in case of a demand decrease.

In either event the actual capital- output ratio diverges from that which had been planned and the actual rate of growth of output therefore diverges from the warranted rate. The actual growth rate is given by the actual savings rate divided by the actual output ratio.

Important consequences follow from these divergences. If producers find that demand in a given period has been higher than the anticipated so that to meet it, in the next period they will increase the investment. However the rise in investment will through multiplier generate a further increase in demand. Once again capacity will prove inadequate and actual output ratio will be higher than the planned capital output ratio. The economy in other words having diverged from the state of steady growth now moves further and further away from that state along an explosive growth path.

If circumstances in which the initial divergence is due to decline in the rate of growth of demand exactly the opposite will occur with net investment falling and eventually becoming negative.

Harrod assumes not only a constant output ratio but also a constant capital-labor ratio and given this assumption the economy cannot at full employment grow faster than the rate of growth of growth of labor force (C/n)

C/n which Harrod terms as the natural rate of growth is the maximum rate of growth allowed by population growth and labor saving technical innovation combined. If either carry actual growth rate or warranted growth rate exceed natural growth rate then at full employment either or both will no longer be realized. If actual growth rate is lowered than in the next period investment plans will be revised downwards. Through the multiplier the string down in investment will lead to a decline in the rate of growth of demand.

Investment plans in the next round will be further contracted and the economy will move into recession. Recession in turn is brought to a halt because at a certain point dis-saving will slow down the decline in consumption as households try to maintain certain minimum standards.

With the slowing down or a halt to the decline in consumption producers who have been idle once again begin to replace worn out equipment. The increased employment in the capital goods sector demand still rises further and once more the process is reversed.

In his view the likelihood that an economy grows steadily at full employment is extremely low. This would require that with the economy already at full employment

$G_w = G_a = G_n$

If the economy is below full employment it is not enough for these inequalities to hold. If they do, full employment will never be reached. For that to occur actual growth rate which may or may not be equal to warranted growth rate must exceed natural growth rate until unemployed labor force is absorbed but if the actual growth rate exceed natural growth rate then full employment is reached. It is unlikely that the triple equality will suddenly hold.

Any divergence of G_a and G_W will lead the economy from the steady growth path.

Harrod observes that the empirical evidence for the U.K suggests that the warranted rate of growth exceeds the natural rate. Thus even if warranted growth rate equals actual growth rate below full employment cyclical swings in economic activity are inevitable. Unless government policy can bring growth rates into line at full employment, $G_a = G_W = G_n$ (they should be equal).

Harrod therefore advocates lowering the warranted rate. On this he recommends use of a low interest rate policy which should lower the inducement to save and to raise the planned capital output ratio by cheapening the price of capital to labor. He advocates for an anti cyclical programs of public works in order to raise the flow of economic recessions. These are not sufficient conditions to achieve steady growth at full employment. They are therefore designed however both to raise the possibility of achieving these and to reduce the degree of fluctuations in economic activities.

In a separate article published in 1947, Evsey Domar reached similar conclusions to Harrods. Hence $g = s/v$ is generally referred to as Harrod Domar model. In this model, the savings rate together with the capital output ratio is reinstated as one of the key determinants of economic growth.

CHAPTER FIVE

TECHNOLOGY AND DEVELOPMENT

5. Introduction

The concern to build models which allowed long run growth in output per head led to a focus on technical progress which came to be seen as a source of long run growth. Technical progress act simply like an expansion of labor force.

For most part in the 1950's and 1960's technical progress was seen as exogenous.

There were however notable examples such as Kaldor (1957), Arrow (1962), Atkinson and Stiglite (1969) where experience was seen as a basis for learning.

There was also a group of papers in which the direction of technical progress was determined by economic choices. Solow in 1957 showed how growth could be composed using an aggregate production function with contributions from different sources namely; the growth rates of factor inputs weighed by computative factor shares plus residual.

$$Gy = W_k. g_k + W_L + g_L + W_R + g_R + a$$

Where a is residual.

This residual was openly called technological progress, although it is perhaps best seen as what it is that is the difference between growth of inputs and a weighted sum of growth of inputs or by definition the growth in total factor productivity.

Whereas a decomposition was suggestive, it was unsatisfactory from the point of view of explaining growth since it is left a major part of sorts of growth to be explained exogenously by technology progress.

Models followed in which the advance of the productivity of factors of production was endogenous. The most important example being that of Arrow (1962) incorporating learning by doing.

There is a different class of models which can explain endogenously the long run rate of growth following the tradition of shell (1975) and more recently Romer (1990) and Lucas (1988).

Technical progress comes from a sector which produces productivity enhancing ideas. The crucial endogenous variable is then the amount of resources which are located to that sector.

Ideas produced by that sector may be used at zero cost in resources by firms in other sectors which produces output of the good which may be consumed or invested. The resources allocated to the ideas sector may be determined in an optimal plan derived from a model for the intertemporal allocation of consumption or from the equilibrium allocation of a market economy. Without intervention, the market outcome will not be optimal because ideas will be generated privately only if their dissemination is limited by for example patents; thus allowing those who generate ideas to sell them for a positive price. Without restrictions such as patents no one will pay for an idea which was freely available to everybody. In these circumstances there is a room for state intervention to increase flow of ideas. This could take place for example through government funding.

There are problems with this approach, however if we try to tell empirical stories. It is extremely difficult to identify anything approximating to a knowledge producing sector in real economies. Research and development activity for example is poorly defined and difficult to interpret and in many cases in practice probably contains little real research.

These newer theories have not provided advance residual or growth in total productivity together or separately. We are faced with identification problem of major proportions.

There is a trade off between consumption today and knowledge that can be used to produce more consumption tomorrow, (Romer 1986, p.1015). He formalizes the mentioned idea in terms of research and technology to produce more consumption tomorrow. Discoveries are made and important in production firms.

5.1. The classical growth theory

Among the classical economists the four most original contributors were Adam Smith, Ricardo, Malthus and Carl – Max prior to the founding of the classical school another group of economists had earlier in the 18th century also studied the process of economic growth.

In France the physiocrats analyzed the scope of advances in both total output per worker including that these could only be generated by agricultural sector. Only labor employed in the exploitation of land was capable of generating surplus output in excess of the value of material inputs and labor employed. Expanded agricultural output leads in turn to increased

supply of food and raw materials to other branches of the economy permitting an expansion of manufacturing output but manufacturing itself could never generate economic growth.
For artisans add to their raw materials only the value of their own labor. From work of Adam Smith the founding father of the classical school onwards, there is recognition that a growth dynamic can be generated in manufacturing as well as agriculture. Agricultural sector can generate advances not only in total output but also in labor productivity. The classical indeed perceived the scope of productivity advances to be greater in manufacturing than in agriculture. These developments in perception were associated with the articulation in a number of prepositions concerning the causes of growth, some of which were completely new and with a new elaboration of the constraints.

5.2. Adam Smith

Adam Smith observed the growth process as purely endogenous, as supported by [Lowe,(1954), 1987,p 108, and Eltis, 1984 p.69). When Adam Smith published the Wealth of Nations in 1776, agricultural and industrial revolutions were both already under way in Britain. At the time Smith was writing he also observed that producers in parts of Europe had been and were experiencing an expansion and extension of markets both domestic and foreign. Two factors, improvement in law and order along actual and potential trade routes and expansion of low cost water transport were resulting in exchange over long distances.

To Smith it is the extension of the market which both makes growth possible and simultaneously providing the necessary inducement not only to expand production but to do so in the mode which increases labor productivity. Extension of the market provides opportunities for increase in the division of labor. The division of labor or specialization rises labor productivity for 3 reasons;

a) It makes workers to be more efficient in performance of particular tasks.
b) Job specialization reduces time wastage while on switching on to new tasks.
c) Job Specialization improves the scope for designing improved tools and machines so as to raise labor productivity.

However while market expansion provides the opportunity for growth in output and labor productivity the latter will only occur if firms respond to new opportunities by committing increased resources to production. It is noteworthy that of Smith's three routes to increased labor productivity only 1/3 is necessarily predicted upon investment in capital equipment. All the three however require that firms mobilize additional working capital in order to take an additional unit of labor. Capital accumulation is therefore necessary for economic growth. However, before an expanded outlay on production can occur, there must be prior increase in savings. Increased savings can only be achieved by those groups in society who have sufficient incomes. Smith identified 3 such groups. These include landlords, merchants and manufactures.

However Smith typical of classical economists did not expect the landlords to constitute a major source of productive investment. As a traditional landlord class spends its income on consumption of commodities and on the hiring of unproductive labor like entertainers. In contrast the landlords, manufactures and merchants out of past profits and in pursuit of their own increased gain, can be expected to generate the bulk of savings that are needed to exploit new markets.

The scope of increasing labor productivity through specialization is much greater through manufacturing. In agriculture the seasonal sequence of tasks makes it impossible to develop enterprises in which different workers are simultaneously engaged upon the various stages of the production process. However there is some scope of productivity increase both for land and labor in this sector through technical innovations for example improved rotation and increased use of fertilizers and through provision of greater incentives to farmers.

Smith in contrast to phsiocrats saw the urban sector which its merchant and manufacturing classes as the leading dynamic sector in economic growth in cotemporally Europe.

At some distant point in future growing economies might reach a point where all scope for the development of their productive capacity would have been exhausted given their natural resources and opportunities for international trade. However Smith did not see the attainment of a stationary state by the growing economies of Western Europe as eminent nor did he analyze any detail, the factors likely to bring it about.

From the analysis of the causes and sources of economic growth, Smith generated policy recommendations geared to sustaining this process.

Government should eliminate all abstructions to free trade and competition.

Controls on international trade and government creation and protection of monopolies should be abolished.

Law and order should be enforced.

5.3. Malthus

In an essay on the principle of population written in 1798, Malthus shows himself to be more concerned of what could be expected to happen over time to mass welfare in an economy than with economic growth. These concerns were probably prompted by co temporally events in particular for the proposal to revise laws so as to give the poor the larger allowances to families with more children.

Malthus is based on a mixture of arguments and factual assertion the essence of which may be summarized as follows;

Economic growth promotes increased demand for labor and hence rising wages. Rising wages in turn lead to an increase in population and hence labor supply with an increase in living standards. Parents choose to have more children and in addition higher proportion of children survive infancy.

These points were commonly made by the classical economists.

The distinctive feature of Malthus thesis is as follows;

Malthus asserted that any rise in the mass living standards could only be temporally because increase in population would rapidly outstrip the capacity of agricultural sector to meet the growing demand for food. For additional land brought into cultivation is generally less fertile than that not cultivated. It is in this context that Malthus made his famous but unsubstantiated assertion that population grows in a geometric progression i.e by a constant proportion with time period. Output can only grow in an arithmetic progression i.e by absolute amount per given period of time.

Malthus took the view that a rise in wages and mass living standards followed by a period of population explosion could only be succeeded by one of growing food shortages and mass misery. This would in turn result in decline in both death rate and infant survival until as a result in decline in population growth, labor shortages emerge and a cycle repeats itself.

The only acceptable way out of this problem was for the working class to exert greater restraint on family size but Malthus did not anticipate this happening. He concluded that only in a society with an equal distribution of wealth and income with some people persistently enjoy high standard of living. In a society with equal income and wealth distribution all would experience periods of fluctuating wellbeing and misery.

Malthus does not provide any sound justification for his proposition concerning the respective growth rates of population and agriculture.
Ricardo in contrast undertook a more sophiscated analysis both of the constraints to agricultural growth and of the impact of these constraints upon the rest of the economy.

5.4. Ricardo

Ricardo like all the classical economists observed that economic growth is financed out of profits accruing from productive activities. If growth is to continue it follows that the share of profits in national income must remain positive.

Ricardo foresaw that a phase of economic growth, profits might quickly be eroded to such an extent that growth itself will be brought to a stationary state. Ricardo argument which begins on the same lines as Malthus was as follows:

Economic growth leads to an increase in demand for labor which in turn lead to a rise in wages and consequently an increase in population. Both arguments generate an increase in demand for food. Ricardo however then produces his own analysis of the consequences of rising food demand.

Ricardo starting point is the fact that in every country land supply is fixed. It is also of a variable quality. At any point in time farmers meet agricultural demand by cultivating the better land and avoiding less good land as much as possible. However as demand increases it is necessary to increase the total area cultivated by bringing less good land under cultivation. Thus marginal cost increase as output increases and profit rates are lowered. Concerning diminishing returns, Ricardo put it that as capital accumulates and population grows and assuming the real wage rate of workers given and constant, the rate of profit is bound to fall; due to extensive and intensive diminishing returns on land (Ricardo 1951, p.98).

Ricardo however identified two possible ways out of this problem. These were the introduction of technical innovations in agriculture and use of international trade to obtain lower cost food in exchange for manufactured goods.

If one or both of these conditions are prevailing, then growth may continue while real wages remain buoyant as a result of rising demand for labor.

5.5. Robert Torrens

In his *Essay on the external Corn Trade,* Torrens emphasized that the concept of surplus provides the key to an explanation of the rate of profit. In his model, 'corn model', the rate of profit can be determined by as the ratio of two quantities of corn: the surplus product and the corn advanced as seed and as food in the support of workers (Torrens, 1820, p.361). Having realized to have ignored the Ricardo's original and profound inquiry into the laws by which profit is determined. In his *Essay on the Production of Wealth*, he published a year later, the surplus and the social capital consisted of the same commodities in the same proportions, so that the rate of profit can be determined without having recourse to the system of relative prices (Torrens, 1821, pp 372-3). Torrens emphasized that the physical schema of the production of commodities is important for both determining the rate of profit and relative prices and providing the basis to assess the growth potential of the economy. The surplus in each sector is used for accumulation purposes, thus determining the expansion of that sector.

5.6. Carl Max

He considered the ideal state for all societies to be one of the material abundancy in context of communal ownership of the means of production where all individuals work according to their ability for the good of society and are rewarded according to their need. He considered that no society had yet achieved this state.

To attain it, it would require the social, political and economic transformation of society. Furthermore to achieve such transformation the society would already have reached a certain level of development of forces and relations of production and of the state apparatus to sustain it.

Marx identified 5 modes of production; the Asiatic, Ancient (slave), feudal, modern capitalistic and communist.

In first four (pre communist modes of production, it is possible to distinguish 2 components of output. i.e the part that is used to sustain the work force and the surplus appropriated from the workers by the dominant class. Appropriation is legislated through the rights of slave ownership, land ownership, ownership of other means of production and through taxation and other forced levies.

In the pre capitalistic modes, the dominant class after meeting subsistence needs uses the surplus or luxury consumption to support the state apparatus and public works of unproductive nature e.g. the monument of Egypt and churches and cathedrals of Europe.

Given these forms of use of this surplus there is no inbuilt tendency to economic growth in these modes and if technical change occurs it does so slowly.

Capitalism differs from all three pre capitalist modes in a number of important respects;

- The objective of production.
- The use made of the surplus by the capitalist class.
- Capitalist inherent drive due to technological progress.
- Its tendency to increase both the socialization and alienation of labor and its inherent tendency to periodic crisis of overproduction and under consumption.

In this model the means of production are owned by the capitalistic class whose dominant objective is not to produce, use values but to accumulate wealth in form of exchange value. This objective determines the use of the surplus which now becomes transformed into surplus value and it gives to capitalism a dynamic input not possessed by previous modes .

It is through the terms of hire of labor that capitalists are able to generate surplus value. The surplus extraction occurs as follows:

- The exchange value of a commodity has three components;

$C + V + S$.

C represents the value of material capital that is used in production. Clearly the full value of C must form part of the value of the finished good if production is to be commercially valued. Meanwhile V represents the cost of labor and for the same reason it must be reflected in the value of the finished good. The value of V is partly determined physiologically and partly socially determined.

Wages must be at least sufficient to permit the survival and physical reproduction of labor. However social convention may set wages at somewhat higher level.

Finally S arises as follows;

Each worker has to work a certain number of hours to produce the value of his wage. Thus requiring labour to work each day for longer than this the capitalist generates the surplus value. The ratio S/V , Carl Max defines it as the rate of exploitation of labor.

Under capitalism, 2 classes with opposing interest dominate economic activity i.e capitalists and proteriat. The more powerful of these classes are the capitalists also dominate the state and uses state institutions to promote its own interests. The driving need of capitalists class to constantly enlarge its wealth leads inevitably to the creation of the preconditions for the transactions to socialism.

The capitalists' objective of surplus accumulation through production and exchange leads capitalists to compete against each other for available markets striving to increase their market shares by undercutting or buying out weaker competitors. There is thus inbuilt tendency towards centralization of capital.

One instrument of competition is the constant search of technical innovations that plays a big role in lowering production costs. Such technical change tends to be associated with enlargement of plant size combined with specialization of labor.

Meanwhile the anarchy of capitalist competition where individual firms expand output without any central coordination and collaboration leads to periodic crises of overproduction and under consumption. Crises may also be caused by a decline in the rate of profit due to capital intensification and increasing labor scarcity and rising wages. During these periods of crises weaker firms collapse or are bought out by stronger ones.

Every time there is a crisis of capitalism labor is laid off and there is a tendency of wages to fall. Consequently in the stronger firms which survive, the initial rise in cost or drop in the rate of profits tends to rise again. Employers may also try to raise the rate of surplus per worker by forcing labor to work longer hours for the same wage. This process leads jointly to the replacement of competitive capitalism by monopoly capitalism.

Meanwhile the development of the productive forces under capitalism, the enlargement of the plant size and increasing specialization of labor lead in turn to increased awareness on the part of the workers of their mutual interdependence in production.

Ultimately a fresh and particularly deep crisis with an associated widespread loss of employment will lead the proteriat to rise up and lease both the means of production and state power from the capitalist class establishing a socialist workers state. In this the ground work will be laid for the transition of a communist society.

5.7. Neo-Classical Model

Geometric Exposition

Solow.

This is one of the simplest growth possible models which assumes that production requires the use of 2 factors of production, labor and capital which are employed in a production function that is subject to constant returns to scale and diminishing returns to increases in the ratio of one factor to the other.

It works under the following assumptions;

a) Labor grows at a constant percentage rate.
b) And that savings equals investments and is a constant fraction of income.

S = s Y

On these assumptions particularly that of constant returns to scale which enables output per factor and the

marginal products of factors to be expressed as functions of the ratios of factors. The economics of growth can be summarized in the diagram below;

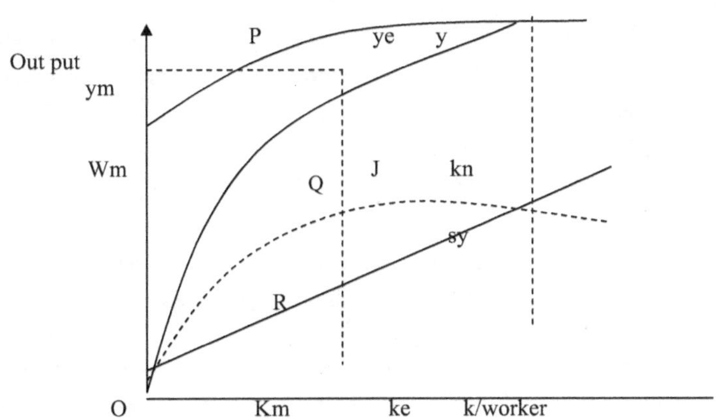

The x – axis represents capital per worker while the y- axis represents output and other magnitude / worker. Oy graphs output per worker as a function of capital per worker.

OSY graphs savings per head as a function of capital per worker.

OKn with slope n which is the rate of population growth rate graphs the investment required to supply the new additions to the labor force with the same capital per head as the existing labor force.

The first preposition to be established is that the economy will converge in the long run on a rate of growth equal to the rate of labor force. To prove this it is sufficient that the economy will converge on an equilibrium stock of capital per head since output per head is constant. The total output must grow at the same rate as the number of heads.

As the diagram shows, there will be such equilibrium stock of capital per head such that savings per head is just sufficient to equip the new workers with the same stock of capital per man as the existing workers possess. This equilibrium stock OKe is indicated by the intersection of OSY with OKn at T.

Suppose that the economy began with the stock of capital per head represented by Km, less than the equilibrium stock Ke, with this stock, output would be KmP or OYm and savings will be KmQ.

KmP would be sufficient to equip the additional workers with the same capital per man as the existing workers so that QR would be available to increase capital per head. Thus capital per head would increase above above OKm and would continue to do so until it reached OKe.

Similary if capital per head is above OKe savings would be insufficient to equip the additional laborers with the same capital per head as the existing laborers command and capital per head would fall to OKe.

Thus T represents a stable equilibrium. But the existence and stability of this equilibrium derive from 2 assumptions implicit in the diagram that; there are sufficiently diminishing returns in production and that at some output per head savings is more than sufficient to equip new workers with the capital per head available to the existing workers.

In the analysis just represented income per head OYeKe and consumption per head Yet are determined given the growth rate of labor force by the saving ratio and can be regarded as a function of that ratio. While income per head rises, as capital per head rises, consumption per head first rises and then declines as capital per head rises. There is a desire for the savings ratio which will maximize consumption per head. This is the ratio for which the long run equilibrium capital stock per head is such that the slope of a tangent to the OY curve at that point is equal to the slope of the OKm curve so that a small variation of the capital labor ratio in either direction does not alter consumption per head and a larger variation in either direction will reduce it.

The maximum consumption per head situation in the diagram is represented by PR. The savings ratio required to achieve it being RKm/PKm.

The behavior requirements for achieving maximum consumption per head may be defined in two alternative ways;

1. The slope of OKn is n. this equilibrium rate of growth of the economy and the slope of OY at P is the marginal product of capital. Hence the condition for maximum consumption can be expressed as equalizing of the rates of return on capital with the growth rate.
2. The savings per head required to maintain the maximum consumption per head measured by RKm. The savings ratio required being RKm/PKm. The income earned by the capital stock perhead is YmWm and the share of capital in output is YmWm/OYm. Since WmYm is equal to RKm, the condition of maximum consumption can be expressed as equality of savings with income of capital or of savings ratio with the share of capital in income. This condition noted and will be filled automatically if as it is assumed by a number of writers on growth theory capitalist save all their income and workers consume all theirs.
3. The condition for maximum consumption per head expressed in the second form has designated as the golden rule of accumulation.

Relaxations of the assumptions

a) the savings assumption; the assumption that the constant proportion of income is saved is completely arbitrary; not can it be defended on the empirical argument of consistency with the observed circular constancy of the ratio of savings to income. The model can however readily be extended in this direction if so desired.

The modification required relate only to the constinction of the savings capital per head relationship and take the advantage of the fact that the distribution of income between the sectors is uniquely related to the capital- labor ratio through the form of the production function. This relationship can be expressed in terms of elasticity of substitution is greater than unity, the share of capital will rise as the capital- labor ratio rises and consequently so will the ratio of savings to income on the assumption of a higher savings ratio out of capital income than output of labor income.

b) Depreciation: relaxation of the assumption that income accumulated lasts forever rises no serious difficulties. The simplest assumption is that capital depreciates by evaporation. A certain fraction of the existing stock disappearing at each moment of time. Thus replacement requirements are a constant fraction of the stock. The model is represented in the diagram below.

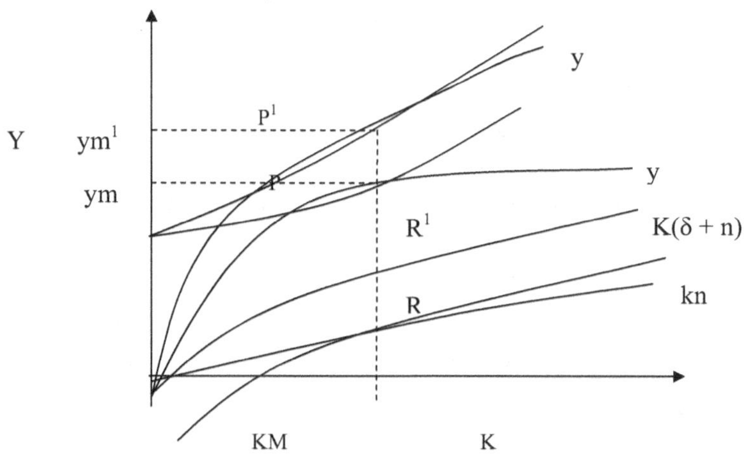

OKm as before represents the net savings required to equip the additional labor resulting from the growth of labor force with the same capital per head as the existing workers. K(δ+n) represents the growth savings required to make depreciation of the existing stock and equip new workers with the same capital as the existing workers. OY represents growth output as a function of capital- labor ration. Oy represents net output after allowance of depreciation.

c) . Technical change: the model assumes only one source of economic growth to which the economy adjusts . i.e. the rate of population increase and does not allow for the possibility of growth through exogenous technical change occurs at a constant rate but that it may be neutral biased towards labor saving or towards capital saving. Neutrality of saving is defined in two major ways;

i. Hicksian neutrality are defined as innovation that raises the marginal productivity of both factors in the same proportion.

ii. Harrod neutrality defined as innovation that at a constant rate of return on capital will keep the capital output ratio constant and raise output per man at the same rate as technical progress occurs.

A diagrammatic model can easily be extended to take account of technical progress of the Harrod neutral type since such progress can be equated to an increase in the effective supply of labor (the equality of labor measured in its efficiency units) at a rate equal to the rate of technical progress.

A notable challenge by some studies such as Acenoglu and Zilibotti (2001), Howit and Mayer (2002) is that the latest technology may not be suitable for use in a country with little human capital. This undermines the productivity and efficiency of capital employed.

CHAPTER SIX

ENTRENUERSHIP AND DEVELOPMENT

6.1. Schumpeter Model of entreprenuership

In Schumpeter published the first German edition to his analysis of economic development. In his study Schumpeter breaks with the classical and neo classical growth theories in several key aspects;

Firstly Schumpeter draws a clear distinction between economic growth and development. The former consists of a gradual process of expansion of production that is producing more of the same and using the same methods in order to do so.

Economic development is more dramatic and disruptive process. It consists in Schumpeter's terminology of carrying out (new combinations of productive means) such that either the conditions of production of the existing goods are transformed or new goods are introduced or new sources of supply or new markets are opened up or an industry is reorganized.

In each case innovation is entailed in production methods, products, markets or industrial organization.

Schumpeter characterizes these five aspects of economic development as giving rise to " productive revolutions" a phrase that emphasizes both the transforming aspect of development and the fact that changes of this type tend to cluster together so that development rather than being a smooth continuous process occurs when the system moves to another configuration of circular flow.

A central aspect of Schumpeter analysis in this specification of the three common features which in his view are inherent in most instances of economic development and without which development cannot generally occur. Each of these Schumpeter places in opposition to another element which in his view has an earlier theorization of economic advance being assigned a misplaced importance. These three central features are as follows:

1. The mobilization of existing factors of production and their combination in new ways.
2. Extension of credit which is generally essential in order to provide the necessary command over these factors in the market.

3. The presence of an economic entrepreneur for the initiation of this process of resource mobilization and for carrying it through completion.

For Schumpeter the essential feature of economic development is not the incremental accumulation of new capital but the mobilization of the existing factors for new uses. If new combinations of factors of production are carried out by existing firms or individuals with substantial wealth then a problem of finance may not arise.

The initiators of new combinations may either have the necessary factors or be able to buy them. However Schumpeter argues the situation is usually different,

Firstly new combinations are as a rule embodied in new firms.

Secondary even large firms usually need extra finance to implement this type of innovation. Some finance comes from investors but most is provided by banks and most of it is generated by bank credit creation.

The lending of saving deposits Schumpeter argues is far more significant in financing economic advance than the expansion of the money supply in the banking system. The banker by creating finance capital for particular purposes has himself become a capitalist.

The capitalist provides the finance and carries a risk of economic development but he does not bring it about. This is done by the entrepreneur i.e. someone who has the poor sight to perceive new opportunities and who takes the initiative to pursue them.

He persuades capitalists to provide the necessary finance and uses this to organize a new combination of productive factors. In the absence of individuals who have these innovatory and organizational talents and motivation to use them economic development cannot occur.

In the early stages of individual revolution the entrepreneur and capitalists were usually one and the same person. However in more industrially advanced societies the two functions are generally separated. The role of entrepreneurs openly being fulfilled by company managers or members of board of directors.

Furthermore entrepreneurship is not a full time permanent occupation. It is a function that certain individuals perform at certain points in time.

Thus with Schumpeter the crucial features for economic development are not mobilization of savings by the capitalists to finance the accumulation of more productive capital but the actions of entrepreneurs in mobilizing credit to finance the procurement of the existing factors of production in order to combine them in new ways.

Innovation lies at the heart of development and the innovator is the entrepreneur. In emphasizing that by the 20th century the activities of the entrepreneur and capitalist have been separated.

Schumpeter may be interpreted as simply updating one element in classical theory. However by distinguishing between growth and development and emphasizing the importance of credit creation he distanced himself from the classical economists.

Credit to the entrepreneur may however come with challenges. Quadrini (1999) and Cagetti and Nardi (2003), using the US data and Paulson and Townsend (2004) using Thailand data calibrated a model with credit constraints to understand the correlation between wealth and the probability of becoming an entrepreneur. Buera (2003) put it that the long run correlation between wealth and entrepreneurship is weaker than the short run correlation. The explanation given to the above phenomenon as noted by Skiba (1978), Deaton (1992), Aiyagan (1994) and Carroll (1997) is that those who are credit constrained now want to invest in the future have a very strong incentive to save. Other challenges include high interest rates and lack of collateral security.

6.2. Lewis Model of economic development with unlimited supply of labour

Lewis takes it that an economy of third World nature typically has unlimited supplies of labor at a subsistence wage. Such labor surplus economies can be divided into capitalistic sector and subsistence sector. The former is very small while the latter is very large. The capitalistic sector is that part of the economy which uses reproducible capital.

The capitalist higher wage laborers are capitalist production that occurs in mines, plantations The subsistence sector in contrast does not use reproducible capital, an output per head is consequently much lower. It is also based on family labor rather than hired labor.

Labor transfers within the dual economy i.e moves from the agricultural sector with low or zero marginal product to capitalist modern industrial sector. Labor is available to the capitalist sector at a wage rate that is determined by earnings in the subsistence sector. Since individuals in this sector generally work in household enterprises and pool their earnings with other household members, their effective income reflects the average rather than income of household members. It is this average income that is the material opportunity cost to a laborer of moving from the subsistence to the capitalistic sector.

The wage rate set by the capitalist sector is at the level of this opportunity cost plus a margin which is just sufficient to enduce workers to move into wage employment.

Lewis central problem is to identify the causes of and constraints to growth. The fundamental constraint to growth in output for Lewis is lack of accumulation of productive capital and the overriding constraint to capital accumulation in his view as that of the classical economists, the rate of saving.

Lewis rejects the possibility that this increase in saving could occur simply because of the population as a whole become thrifty. This is not plausible partly because 90% of the population in poor countries with surplus labor never manages to save a significant proportion of its income; and secondary because in underdeveloped countries a substantial proportion of the rich are land owners. These have a high marginal propensity to consume out of rental incomes and even when rentals are saved, they are usually used unproductively. E.g buying new assets rather than creating new incomes.

Lewis assumes in classical tradition that capitalist profits are saved and invested. The question then becomes, what are the circumstances under which the share of the profits in national income increases because in these circumstances the share of the savings will also increase.

Lewis constructs a model of the closed economy which is intended to throw light on the nature of this process. Where the capitalist nucleus exists however small and where there is unlimited supply of cheap labor then the capitalists will re invest at least part of their profits and thus expanding the capital stock.

With the wages in the capitalistic sector remaining at the subsistence level, the share of profits in national income rises as the capitalistic sector expands. As the share of profits rises the share of savings and investment in national income rises too; thereby increasing the rate of economic growth.

This is the process that Lewis illustrates in the figure.

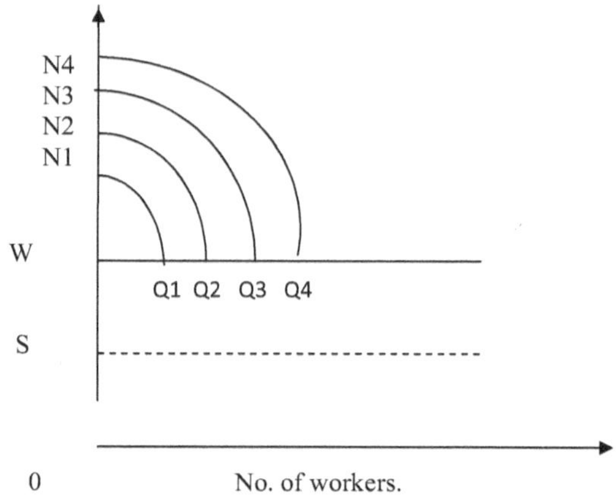

In the figure OS is the average sub earnings.

OW is the capitalist wage.

NQ is the schedule of marginal product of labor.

W_1NQ_1 represents the surplus initial stage. Since some of this is reinvested the total amount of fixed capital increases hence the schedule of marginal productivity of labor is raised to the level N_2Q_2.

Both the surplus and capitalist employment are now larger. Further investment raises the schedule of marginal productivity to N_3Q_3 and the process continues as long as there is surplus labor.

Having set up which model of expanding capitalist nucleus Lewis considers certain factors that may aid or impede its expansion.

Lewis shows that in certain circumstances expansion of monetary supply and price inflation can accelerate economic growth in a country with surplus labor. This can occur when credit is created in favor of private capitalists or when it used to finance government capital provided that the projects financed generate increased output fairly quickly.

Further there are however three factors that may constrain the effectiveness of monetary expansion as a growth promoter;

1) If prices rise too fast or too slow investors, may lose confidence and turn to various forms of unproductive investment e.g. speculation of commodities and large purchase.
2) The smaller the class of the capitalist the greater the likelihood that much of the expanded money supply will find its way into the pockets of other groups.
3) In an open economy expansion of the monetary demand would put pressure on the balance of payments position.

He also notes that it is a natural tendency of governments to try to control price inflation and to do so by fixing industrial price. However in an inflation context government should not control industrial prices since it is industrial capitalist class which saves most. Industrial price controls reduce profits and therefore savings and investments.

Lewis offers what is predominantly rather account of the steady expansion which he equates with economic development. However he also shows that the working population cannot expect immediate rise in the living standards if capitalist growth is to be maximized. Meanwhile capitalist growth may be slowed down by capital outflow.

Another concern noted by economists is the effect of the price system in the rewards for labor for example, even if there are different education levels and skills, the wage payoff to such level will be determined by the market forces. There is a good reason to argue (see, e.g., Ljung (1993), Freeman (1996) and Mookherjee and Ray (2002b, 2003) that the price system sort individuals into different occupational choices, and therefore persistent inequality inequality across dynasties located at each of these occupational slots. This poses a disadvantage to those who are trapped in lower levels due low education, ill health, low nutrition among other factors that places these individuals in occupational choices that are not adequately rewarding.

CHAPTER SEVEN

7.1. Rostow's stages of economic growth

For Rostow like Lewis a crucial factor which serves to lift an economy out of low income stagnation on to a sustained growth path is a significant increase in the share of savings and investment of national income. For this to occur a new class of entrepreneurs must emerge.

Rostow attempts to give a rather precise time perspective to this process to establish the nature of the main political, social and institutional changes which form an integral part of it.

During the take off period new enterprising men come forward willing to take risks in pursuit of profits for example in commerce, markets widen, basic capital is expanded notably in transport and communication often to bring to market raw materials in which other nations an economic interest.

Financial institutions develop to support this increased activity and here and there modern manufacturing enterprise usually in substitution for imports.

During the pre- take off phase, the rate of productive investment may rise up to 5% of the national income. This phase is followed by take off into self sustaining growth during which the rate of investment increases in such away that real output per capita rises and this initial increase carries with it radical changes in production technique.

The take off requires therefore a society prepared to respond actively to new possibilities for productive enterprise and it is likely to require political, social and institutional changes which will both perpetuate an initial increase in the scale of investment and result in the regular acceptance and absorption.

The beginning of take off can usually be traced to a particular sharp stimulus. The stimulus may take the form of political revolution or technological innovation or newly favorable international environment e.g. opening of British and France markets for Swedish timber in 1860's but it may also come as a challenge posed by a favorable shift in the international environment such as a sharp fall in terms of trade requiring rapid development of manufactured import substitutes.

Rostow observes that while national income aggregates reveal little of the essential underlying changes, it is nevertheless useful to regard as a necessary but not sufficient condition for the take off the fact that the proportion of net investment to national income rise from 5% to over 10% definitely outstripping the likely population pressure.

7.2. The concept of the leading sector.

In an attempt to disaggregate the nature of both processes, Rostow analyses the interrelationship between the growth performance of different sectors introducing the concept of the primary or leading sector which plays a key role both during the take off and subsequent stages. Thus the sectors of an economy may be grouped into 3 categories;

a. Primary growth sectors; where possibilities for innovation or for exploitation of newly profitable unexplored resources yield a high growth rate and they set in motion expansion process elsewhere in the economy.
b. Supplementary growth sectors; where a rapid advance occurs in direct response to or as a requirement of an advance in the primary growth sectors.
c. Derived growth sectors; where advance occurs in some fairly steady relation to the growth of total real income, population, and industrial production for example food output in relation to population, are classic derived relations to this order.

At any period of time it appears to be true even in a mature and growing economy that forward momentum is maintained as a result of rapid expansion in a limited number of primary sectors whose expansion has significant external economy and other secondary effects.

Like the take off long term growth requires that the society not only generate vast quantities of capital for depreciation and maintenance but also a sequence of highly productive primary sectors growing rapidly based on new production functions.

To achieve satisfactory growth in balance with the rising demand in the derived growth sector requires a diffusion of technical innovations in these sectors too. Examples of leading sectors in the take off include the textile industry in Britain, railway development in U.S.A, Germany and France, the timber industry in Sweden and armaments production for rapid militarization in Russia.

Liu, Z (2008) emphasizes how foreign direct investment generates externalities in form of technology transfer that has an effect of productivity of domestic firms. This boosts the export sector and there improved balance of payments position.

CHAPTER EIGHT

TRADE AND DEVELOPMENT

8.1. NORTH- SOUTH Un-equal Exchange

Prebisch (1950) put forward the view that the terms of trade of the developing countries tend to deteriorate over time. Prebisch tries to explain such adverse movement of the terms of trade against LDCs by the following factors;

1) The trade unions in developed countries are more capable of raising wages for their workers than the trade unions in LDCs which are frequently very weak.
2) The increase in population in LDCs and the consequent rise in the labor supply has been absorbed mainly in those sectors where the labor productivity is quite low and this has also resulted in a lower level real wages.

Singer also argued that another reason both for down ward long term trend in the terms of trade for primary products and for expecting only relatively low growth of future primary export volume outlay in the different income elasticities of demand for primary and industrial products. These being generally low for the former and higher for the latter.

Another reason noted by Murksa (1957) was development in the industrially advanced countries of synthetic substitutes for the primary products. Prebisch in 1964 emphasized both these factors and in addition the further depressing effects on demand for primary exports from the periphery of growing protectionism in European agriculture and increased efficiency in the industrial economies in the use of raw materials leading to less input per unit of output.

Evaluation of this sythesis

Mier argues that the import price index conceals heterogeneous price movements within and among the broad categories of food stuffs, raw materials and minerals and no allowance is made for changes in the quality of exports and imports. There is inadequate consideration of new commodities and the recorded terms of trade are not corrected for the substantial decline in transport costs. The introduction of new products and qualitative improvements have been greater in manufactured than primary products.

Even if it were true that the LDCs experienced a secular deterioration in the commodity terms of trade the question would still remain whether this constituted a significant obstacle to their development. The answer depends on what caused the deterioration and whether the country's factoral terms of trade can improve at the same time. As long as productivity in its export industries is increasing more rapidly than the fall in the export prices the country's real income can rise despite the deterioration in the commodity terms of trade.

Another criticism leveled against Prebisch study on the trends of terms of trade during 1950's concerns the selection of the base year, it is hardly surprising that the subsequent trend is down wards, since was a year of very high primary products prices associated with the outbreak of the Korean war. Likewise when the mid 1870's are selected as a base the long term trend in the commodity terms of trade for primary products again appears to be down ward until mid 1930's.

Conversely when 1900 is taken as a base year a number of analysits have found no clear trend on the basis of long term information.

Lipsey (1963) has shown that the terms of trade have actually moved in favor of LDCs visa vis USA and Europe. But during the same period starting with the last quarter of the 18th century the terms of trade have moved against LDCs visa vis UK.

Discussions about terms of trade are inconclusive in one way or the other since the results crucially depend upon the base period.

At the theoretical level it has been argued that Prebisch notion that the gains from technological progress should be distributed globally independent of the countries of their origin is of doubtful of validity. If such a distribution of gains means equalization of global real wages then the realities of the present world like the trade barriers which rule out the factor price equalization and will also rule out any such global equalization of real wages.

Also gains from technological progress could emerge from the expenditure on research and development. And such gains are not for free global distribution. So the value judgment about their equal distribution has been questioned.

CHAPTER NINE

HUMAN RESOURCES AND ECONOMIC DEVELOPMENT

9. Case study: Uganda

Human resource development goes hand in hand with economic progress. Douglas Massey (1995) asserts that without a sustained and economic progress at the individual as well as society level, achievement of human resource potential would not be possible.

For Uganda's case, soon after independence in 1962 the first 5 year development plan was launched. Education was the first social priority because of its wide geographical impact, importance of education and greater demand for education. The long term educational goals was to achieve universal education.

During this period there was a rapid extension of higher education with the aim of Ugandanising the civil service. There was also expanded provision of education for girls and practical skill building through farm schools and technical schools.

Health was the second priority because of heavy toll of diseases. The long term health policy was to provide a comprehensive national health service to all citizens although it required substantial economic growth to achieve the goal.

The weakness of the system.

- Over centralization of power by the central government.
- Excessive control of the government over people's organizations for example marketing cooperatives and trade unions. This left private individuals with no extra cash to spend on human development. All these problems hindered promotion of human development.

However successive regimes significantly reduced expenditure on human development in favor of military expenditure.

1971- 1985 PERIOD

This period was characterized by adverse economic and political conditions. The economy was mismanaged and the overall conditions of human existence deteriorated. During this period human development was not a priority.

1986- 1997 PERIOD

The period was characterized by relative stability. The government of Uganda's rehabilitation and development program of 1993- 96 specifying that the development agenda for the 1990's is the provision of basic social services. That agenda was consistent with point 6 of the National Resistance Movement program. The focus was on primary health care, primary education and adult literacy.

9.1. State of Health and Education in Uganda

Education

Education attainment is a key factor in determining a nations medium term growth path. Uganda's standing illiteracy rate in 1992 was 51% compared to 71% in Kenya. The proportion of children between of children between 7-13 years of age in Uganda was 70% and the net urban enrollment for girls was 67% and boys was 73%.

In spite of the poor picture of educational attainment, there has been increased enrollment from 2% in 1992/93 to 3% in 1994/95. In 1997 enrollment in primary schools more than doubled after the introduction of UPE (i.e. from approximately 2.9 million to 5.7 million). However drop outs are high. In 1992, 70% dropped out by primary seven (females 15% and males 64%). In 1986 only 16% of the students of students entering secondary school drop out. By 1991, 47% were dropping out. This imply that more children are entering the school than before but a higher proportion is dropping.

Health

Health indicators in Uganda are very poor. Uganda compared favorably to other sub Saharan countries in 1960's but has since dropped in standing.

Time period(1992)	Uganda	Kenya	Tanzania
Infant mortality.	104	67	103
Life expectancy.	42.6	58.6	52.1
Access to safe water.	15.	50	51

Reasons for poor human state in Uganda

1) Widespread poverty. A recent study indicated that children from poor families have a lower enrollment rate than their counterparts from the rich families. A recent World Bank study also shown that 55% of Ugandans were poor and disproportionate number of this were in rural areas. The East and the north emerged as the poorest regions.
2) The relative poor performance reflects Uganda's break down in the development, and administration in the early 1970's and 80's.
3) Insufficient financing. Since 1970 successive regimes significantly reduced expenditure on social and human development in favor of military expenditure.
4) The reasons of gender differences in educational attainment include; parents have different aspirations for girls and boys. There is evidence that married less likely to remit cash to their parents. Also the community feel that educated girls are also difficult to marry.
5) Economic decline certainly played a major part in decline of health services. But this is not a sufficient explanation because other countries have raised life expectancy even when their incomes were very low.
6) Other reasons for the poor indicators of health include illiteracy and transport problems. This explains the popularity of traditional indicators.

9.2. The linkage between Education and economic development

1. Productivity. Education is essential for raising individual productivity. Educated people use more capital efficiently. Educated people are also more likely to innovate i.e to devise new and better forms of production. Moreover they speed the benefits to their coworkers who learn from them and also become more productive. Thus rising the level of education causes a rise in the efficiency of all factors. Education also leads to occupational specialization.
2. Education leads to mobility of workers. Generally education gives children skills that they can later transfer from one job to another and basic intellectual necessary tools for further learning.
3. Education leads to a more equitable distribution of income. However recent studies indicate that education in developing countries widen the income gap.
4. Education raises the probability of workers to receive training after their formal education. In Peru many workers were 25% more likely to receive training from their employers if they had some rather no secondary schooling. If they had completed secondary education, they were 52% more likely to receive training.

5. Education leads to adoption of new technologies and production practices. Evidence is high yielding varieties of food grown in India and China. In India areas where relatively few farmers had had primary schooling at the onset of the Green revolution experienced less growth than the areas with the same technological opportunities but with better educated harmers.
6. Education leads to changes in customary values and traditional institutions that minimize the incentive for economic change.
7. Studies carried out by Kuznet and Beeker show that a dollar invested in education brings a more and greater increase in national income than a dollar spent on dams, roads, factory, or other tangible capital goods. Research in Uganda has confirmed that primary education (especially the first 4 years) increases agricultural income and reduces poverty and that all levels of education contribute to the reduction of child mortality.
8. A well educated labor force attracts capital investment which may spearhead development increasing the skills and capacity of workers as a key of economic success in an increasing integrated global economy.

Psacharopolous (1973, 1985, 1994, 2002), emphasizes average mincherian returns to education and stresses that these returns are larger in poor countries compared to rich countries. Education in the poor countries is essential for change of attitude, skill acquisition and employment to minimize income gaps, and bringing about social structural information among other benefits.

9. In addition to direct economic returns education is associated with larger externalities than any other social investment. It creates more informal electorate (voters). Havemen and Wolfe (1984) have identified many non market benefits of education including better decisions around the home, better sanitation, more efficient consumption and even better choice of marital partners.

Why human capital may not be a sufficient condition to attain economic development.

1) While international studies have documented the positive impact of education on growth some countries such as Phillipines and Vietnam have built up large stocks of quality human capital but have not enjoyed the economic growth that normally goes with it. To these countries education attainment is necessary but not sufficient condition for economic growth. Macroeconomic stability and export oriented policies are also essential catalyst for development that raise the returns to human capital and investment in education.

2) Human capital can be of poor quality. Poorly trained labor is a waste of human resources.
3) Poor man power planning; No effects may be made to match the demand and supply of different types of critical skills. Few countries can go on absorbing poorly trained labor at a faster rate than their economic growth. Considering the high costs of education, educated who are unemployed are a huge waste of human and material resources. Expansion of human capabilities delivers its full potential only when there is a corresponding increase in market driven demand for labor skills. Bils and Klenow (2000) calibrate a simple neo – classical model. This model requires that the impact of schooling on individual productivity need to be consistent with the average coefficient obtained from mincer regressions.
4) Politicians view investment in human capital in terms of providing buildings and equipments than teaching staff. Excessive expenditure on infrastructure rather than on teaching staff and supplying depresses the quality and quantity of the schooling so do poorly trained teachers who fail to set up high standards for students.
5) Human capital investments can be of many types. Human tends to be relatively unproductive where the skills acquired in school do not the market skills. Human capital can also be poorly used or misallocated.

Different surveys on the correlation between education and growth for example (Barro (1991), Benhabib and Speigel (1994) and Barro and Sala- I-Martin (1995) seem to be high to be entirely explained by the causal effects of transitional differences in human capital growth rates on economic growth rates.

With the liberalization of the Uganda's economy in the service sector, many private schools were put up and this supplemented the government to offer education to the citizens. The number of children going to school and ultimately completing primary level has been steadily increasing over the years.

The table shows Registered candidates (completing primary seven) by ownership from 2010-2012

	GOV'T	GOV'T		PRIVATE	PRIVATE				
Year	**Male**	**Female**	**Total**	**Male**	**Female**	**Total**	**Male**	**Female**	**Total**
2012	255,893	249,677	505,570	29,030	30,140	59,170	284,817	279817	564740
2011	242,958	236,221	479,179	26,334	27,481	53,815	269,292	263702	532994
2010	238,412	228,735	467,147	24,291	25,250	49,541	262,703	253985	516688

Source. UNEB (Uganda National Examinations Board)

From the information in the table, the number of candidates for Primary Laving Examinations between 2010 and 2012 increased from 238,412 to 255,893 candidates (an increase of 9%) for government schools and 8% for private schools.

Also noted was that for government schools, in 2010 the proportion of girls that registered was 49% while boys were 51%. In 2012 the proportions remain almost the same.

On the contrary, though the population numbers in private schools were smaller, the proportion girls to boys is slightly higher from 2010 to 2012, i.e 50.1% girls and 49.1% boys in 2010, 51% girls and 49.1% boys in 2011 while in 2012 there were 50.9% girls and 49.1% boys.

On close examination, and discussions from selected participants, it was found out that most private schools are boarding schools and most parents prefer to take their girls to such schools. Walking long distances possesses a threat to the young girls.

A notable challenge was lack of meals for lunch time that could have contributed to poor grades. Observational studies such as (Jacoby (2002), Long (1991), Powell, Grantham-McGregor and Nelson (1991) assert that school meals is another way to pay children to attend school with increased school participation. Unfortunately most parents have failed to provide food for their children in primary schools and this could have led to pupil demotivation.

9.3. The Impact of AIDS on economic development of Uganda

The AIDS epidemic began to spread in Uganda during mid 1970's. by 1993 an estimated 15% of Uganda's adult population (around 1.3 million people) out of 17 million was infected with AIDS compared to 15 million people that were infected globally. Of these 2/3 (10 million people were from Africa. To many AIDS is a health problem and possesses additional strains on national health systems but as Uganda and other countries have come to realize AIDS is not solely a health problem rather the epidemic will have a far reaching impact on economic development process.

Effects of AIDS include:

1) The immediate impact of AIDS will be through the changes in both quality and the size of the labor force. Not only is the current stock of the educated elite being reduced but the future quality and quantity is likely to be reduced both because the teachers are among the age groups highly affected and because families will have reduced financial resources to pay for school fees. Also AIDS will reduce both the size and growth of labor force.
2) The key features of Ugandan economy and labor market make Uganda particularly vulnerable than potential effects of the AIDS epidemic. The increasing spread of HIV infection in rural areas combined with intensive and relative scarcity of labor in agriculture production suggests that AIDS epidemic is likely to have a negative impact on both overall production and per capita income.
3) AIDS will have long term negative consequences on capital formation which in turn influences overall productivity of the labor force and ultimately economic growth. A society's ability to invest in physical capital will be reduced as expenditures will be diverted to meet increased health care and other expenditures related to AIDS. In addition AIDS will also affect the productivity of labor force as re occurring episodes of HIV related illness impair productivity through reduced functional capacity. In the household other family members including children will allocate some of their time to care for the patient potentially reducing overall household allocation for productive activities in the house, field or market. In the work place other workers may be required to assume responsibilities of ill workers. Also the premature death of persons with AIDS affects productivity b lobbying the economy of experienced workers many of whom are difficult to replace.
4) In a study by Usher (1978) his empirical findings indicated that increases in life expectancy leads to increases in personal income. This is possible because long life spans provide additional incentives to acquire more education and job training. Similarly since AIDS

leads to decreases in life expectancy this may imply that personal incomes will have to decrease because of low educational training.

Despite countries to attain the millennium development goals, Uganda has not achieved enough in AIDS control. Olive (2013) put it that Uganda government fight against HIV/AIDS had not achieved much, with the current prevalent rates at 7.3%, up from 6.4% in 2004 to 2005. Millenium Development goal 6 to combat HIV/AIDS, malaria and other diseases has therefore met several challenges.

9.4. The Uganda's Strategies and policies underlying Human development initiative

The government of Uganda's rehabilitation program from 1993/94 specifies that the development agenda of the 1990's in the provision of basic social services to the entire population. The priorities for development of the social services sector in the 1990's are articulated in the 'Way forward IV' are better known as Uganda national plan of action for children (UNPAC). The plan provides strategies, goals and targets in the priority areas of primary health care. Primary education, safe water all of which are central to human development. UNPAC main focus is the pursuit of improved social conditions especially for children and women who constitute 75% of the population. UNPAC provides the necessary short term program, financial and policy framework meeting the development needs children and women; the most vulnerable portion of the population.

Education

A situation analysis conducted in 1989 revealed poor standards of basic education and high levels of adult illiteracy which was 49%. It noted that poor quality education was to low teacher- pupil ratio, classroom overcrowding and shortage of classroom/ instruction materials. Besides the revalation of the situation analysis poor incentives to school teachers has also eroded their commitment to teaching. In addition the primary school curriculum has tended to be irrelevant to the skills needed by primary school drop outs to adopt the life outside school.

This is part of the situation that UNPAD is responding to. The focus has been basic education intended to equip people with knowledge, skills, attitudes and values necessary to survive and improve the quality of their lives. The major goal is to increase access to primary education from 69% to 95% and completion rate of primary education cycle from 32% to 50%.

It also aims at reducing the rate of illiteracy. Women are particularly targeted with the view of reducing their illiteracy rate from 54% to 24% by the year 2000. Increased earnings improved knowledge of health care and reduction of fertility have been expected as secondary benefits.

Health

Health is an essential need in regard to building human potentials and capabilities. Improved health especially among children and mothers is important in reducing the infant mortality and maternal mortality. Child survival depends on improved health. This calls governments to invest in health for sustained growth and economic development. Macro economics and Health report (2001) estimated the returns of investing in health to be 500% mostly on the basis of cross country gross progressions. Surveys done by (Strauss and Thomas , (1995), Strauss and Thomas (1998), Thomas (2001), and Thomas and Frankenberg (2002) stress the impact of different measures of health on fitness and productivity. This shows the need to plan for health through planning by all the relevant key players so as to achieve sustainable development. Unhealthy population may spend time and resources on ill health as well as having a minimal contribution to the marginal product per unit of labor employed. The population therefore needs proper nutrition, medical care, decent housing, clean and safe water so as to be healthy.

The basic problems being addressed by government are high infant mortality, 122 per 1000 births reported in 1991 census, the high maternal mortality of 1200 per 100000 according to WHO and UNICEF estimates. And prevalence of immunisable and preventable diseases for example diarrhea.

Despite the government's effort to support the elderly for the recent past, they have been left in the situation of total hopelessness with no food, shelter and closing. It is just two years ago when the government of Uganda started on piloting the project of paying sh. 24,000 to each elderly person in the 14 districts of the country. The Members of parliament on social protection have requested government to extend the senior citizens grant to the entire country under a program called Expanding Social Protection (ESP) program. (12th April 17, 2013 Daily Monitor).

AIDS infection is estimated at 6-10% of the country's population. The underlying causes of the health problems are inadequate access of health information, negative attitudes and practices and poor access to quality health care. It also emphasizes community based intervention in health promotion, disease control, sanitation and simple curative and rehabilitation health care. Social mobilization and technical guidance through the local governance systems are widely used to implement the policy. Community participation in decision making, resource mobilization, program implementation and supervision in partnership with health providers is being encouraged.

The health management has been restructured to decentralize decision making to the district level. All the districts draw their health plans. An important aspect of health care delivery is the use of information, education and communication strategies to overcome inadequate knowledge, negative attitudes and practices that hinder development. Messages are developed to provide the population with information needed for behavioral choices related for example to HIV and Sexually Transmitted Diseases control, use of family planning, provision of better nutrition and dealing with preventable and immunisable diseases.

Other notable challenges include lack of access to safe water. According to Wateraid Uganda, 9.3 million people do not access safe water and this greatly impacts on the welfare of the population. (New Vision of 28th March 2013). It also notes that 26,000 children die of diarrhea due to poor sanitation and lack of safe water in Uganda. Lack of safe and clean water results into unhealthy population whose effort to fight poverty is so minimal. Gilbert, K (2013), asserts that lack of clean water and safe sanitation traps multitudes of people in poverty as most sources of income depend on water. Small scale and big manufacturing firms thrive water as one of the production inputs.

CHAPTER TEN

Recommendations

Governments should make water and sanitation a priority while allocating national resources. This is necessary in rural areas where the majority of the population live.

On top of infrastructural development such as building health centres, schools and power generating centers, there is need of all stakeholders such as the politicians, civil society, the masses and government to emphasize the quality service delivery. It is not enough to build schools but also availability of drugs and other facilities in these centres. Quality education in schools provide the population with the required values, skills and attitude that can cause socio economic transformation.

Cooperative movement is necessary so as to promote collective ideas in production, marketing and value addition. The bargaining power of the members is improved and this helps producers to fetch fair prices for their products.

There should be respect, promotion and enforcement of human rights. This entails building structures towards good governance, participatory democracy, and building and deepening understanding among the population especially the vulnerable groups. This help to fight the common problems that affect human condition such as poverty pandemic.

There should be programs towards achieving sustainable livelihoods. These are programs on human security, education, HIV/AIDS, governance and democracy. These maximize program synergy and deepen interventions so as to have an impact on all beneficiaries.

Despite need to involve many stakeholders involvement, a bottom up approach is needed to find ways how poverty, disease, ignorance can be overcome. Political leaders, civil society organizations and government have a role of bringing the people together so that amicable solutions to society are reached.

Public awareness is very important through education programs like workshops, seminars and symposiums to enlighten the masses about democracy, human rights, political economy, advocacy, youth affairs and the disadvantaged and community development. This instills the spirit of hard work, competitiveness, high value judgment and attitudinal change.

There is need to have programs to cater for the escalating unemployment especially among the youth. Many parts of the world especially the sub-Saharan have the fastest growing population with low productivity economic enterprises to cater for the increasing population. The youth are energetic with innovative and creative ideas but not tapped because most of them are not employed in gainful and constructive employment in some parts of the world.

There need for increased governments initiative towards population control through family planning programs. Rural communities should be sensitized on the importance of small families and the need to save and invest. People's mindset should change so that the masses can understand how family planning can improve their lives among other issues. Educating the girl- child can bring about the desired results of bringing the rates of population growth rates lower since the girls will spend more time at school.

One of the notable challenges towards human capital development in some communities is child labor. Under this practice children are denied a chance to go to school and subjected to work which affects them mentally, physically and socially. The unfortunate part of it is that child is increasing; a case of Uganda for example, it has increased from 1.4 million to 2.7 million for the last 4 years (Sunday Vision, 16th June 2013). It is therefore important to condemn child labor with stringent policies so as to have proper human capital development.

References

Abhijit Bernajee and Esther Duflo. Growth Theory through lens of Development Economics. Massachusetts Institute of Technology.

Acenoglu, Daron and Zilibotti (2001). Productivity differences. *Quarterly Journal of Economics* 116(2), 563-606

Aiyagari, S. Rao (1994). Uninsured idiosyneratic risk and aggregate saving. *Quarterly Journal of Economics* 109, 569-684.

Arrow, K.J.(1962). The Economic implications of Learning by Doing, *Review of Economic Studies*, **29**, 155-173.

Azariadis, C. and A. Drazen (1990). Threshold Externalities in Economic Development. *Quarterly Journal of Economics* **105**. 501-26.

Bardhan, P. and C. Udry (1999). *Development Microeconomics*. New York: Oxford University Press.

Barro, Robert J(1991). Economic growth in a cross section of countries. *Quarterly Journal of Economics* 106(2) 407-443

Barro, Robert J and Xavier Sala-I- Martin (1995). Economic Growth. New York: McGraw Hill.

Barro, Robert, J.(2000). Inequality and growth in a panel of countries. *Journal of Economic Growth* 5(1), 5-32

Benhabib and Mark M. Spiegel (1994). The role of human capital in economic development. Evidence from aggregate cross country data. *Journal of monetary economics* 34(2), 143-174

Benhabib, J. and Rustichini (1996). Social Conflict and Growth. *Journal of Economic Growth* **1**, 125- 142.

Bils, Mark and Peter Klenow (2000). Does schooling cause growth? *American Economic Review* 90(5), 1160-1183

Brinley Thomas (1954). *Migration and Economic Growth*. London: Cambridge University.

Buera, Francisco (2003). *A dynamic model of entrepreneurship with borrowing constraints.* USA: Mimco University of Chicago

Cagetti, Marco, and M. De Nardi (2003). Entrepreneurship, frictions and wealth. Staff Report 324, Federal Reserve Bank of Minneapolis.

Carrol, Christopher (1997). Buffer-stock saving and the life cycle/ permanent income hypothesis. *Quarterly Journal of Economics* 112, 1-56.

Carvalho, Ireneu (2000). *Household incomes as a determinant of child labor and school enrolment in Brazil: Evidence from a social security reform.* Mimco. MIT

Cole, Harold, Geaorge Mailath, and Andrew Postlewaite (1992). Social norms, Savings behavior and growth. *Journal of Political Economy* 100(6), 1092-1126

Cole, Harold, Geaorge Mailath, and Andrew Postlewaite (1998). Class systems and the enforcement of social norms. *Journal of Public Economics* 70(1), 5-35

Cole, Harold, Geaorge Mailath, and Andrew Postlewaite (2001). Investment and concern for relative position. *Review of Economic Design* 6, 241-261

Commission on macroeconomics and Health (2001). *Macroeconomic and Health: Investing in health for economic development.* Geneva: World Health Organization.

Daily Monitor (12th April 2013). Kampala.

Dasgupta, P. (1993). *An inquiry into Well- Being and Destitution.* Oxford: Clarendon Press.

Deaton, Angus (1992). *Understanding consumption.* Oxford: Oxford University Press.

Debraj Ray (2007). *Development Economics.* New York University.

DFID, (2004). The importance of financial sector development for growth and poverty reduction. *DFID Policy Division working paper.*

Eltis, W. (1984). *The Classical Theory of Economic Growth.* London: Macmillan. Douglas Massey. The new immigration and ethnicity in the United States. *Population and Development Review* **21** (September 1995): 631-652.

Freeman, S.(1996). Equilibrium Income Inequality among Identical agents. *Journal of Political Economy* 104, 1047-1064.

Gilbert, K(2013). Population growth greatly affecting access to safe water. (New Vision).Kampala.

González, F.(2007). Effective Property Rights, Conflict and Growth. *Journal of Economic Theory*, in press.

Hadjimicheal, et al (1994). Effects of macroeconomic stability on growth, savings and investment in sub-saharan Africa- an empirical investigation. *International Monetary Fund Working Paper* 97/1

Haveman, Robert. H and Barbara Wolfe (1984). Schooling and Economic well being. The role of non-market effects. *Journal of Human Resources* 19(3): 377-407

Heinz D. Kurz & Neri Salvadori, Theories of Economic Growth- Old and new.

Hirschman, A.(1958). *The strategy of Economic Development.* New Haven, CT : Yale University Press.

Hoff, K., Braverman, A. and J. Stiglitz, eds (1993*). The Economics of Rural Organisation: Theory , Practice and Policy.* London : Oxford University Press.

Howit, P., and D. Mayer (2002). R & D, Implementation and stagnation. A Schumpeterian theory of convergence clubs. Working Paper 9104, National Bureau of Economic Research.

Jacoby Hanan (2002). Is there an intra household fly paper effect? Evidence from a school feeding program.*Economic Journal* 112(476), 196-221

Joseph, L. Love.(1980). Paul Prebisch and the origins of unequal exchange. Latin American Research Review 15, 45-72

Kaldor.N.(1957). ' A Model of Economic Growth', *Economic Journal*, **67**, pp 126-50.

Knack, Stephen and Philip Koefer (1995). Institutions and economic performance. Cross country tests using alternative institutional measures. *Economics and Politics* 7(3), 207-227.

La. Grandville (2011). Economic Growth and Development. Emerald Book series and Monographs.

Leibenstein, H.(1957). *Economic Backwardness and Economic Growth.* New York: Wiley.

Liu, Z (2008). Foreign direct investment and technology spill overs: Theory and Practice. *Journal of Development Economics*. Vol.85 Issue 1-2 Feb 2008 pages 176-193.

Ljungqvist, L. (1993). Economic Underdevelopment. The Case of Missing Market for Human Capital.*Journal of Development Economics* 40, 219-239.

Long, Sharon K. (1991). Do school nutrition programs supplement household food expenditures? *Journal of Human Resources* 26, 654-678

Lowe, A. (1954). The Classical Theory of Economic Growth, *Social Research,*21, 127-58.

Reprinted in A. Lowe, *Essays in Political Economics: Public Control in a Democratic Society*, edited by A. Oakley, Brighton 1987: Wheat sheaf Books..

Lucas, R. (1988). On the Mechanics of Economic Development. *Journal of Monetary Economics* 22, 3-42.

Marshal A.(1920). *Principles of Economics*.(8th ed). New York: Macmillan.

Maunder e tal (1996). *Economics Explained*.(3rd edition). Musselburgh: Scotprint Ltd.

Mauro, Paolo (1995). Corruption and growth. *Quarterly Journal of Economics* 110(3), 681-712.

Michael P. Todaro (2003). Economic Development. India: Nutech Photolithographers.

Ministry of Education and Sports Status Report on Primary Laeving and performance of candidates in PLE for the period 2010-2012.

Mookherjee, D. and D. Ray (2001). *Readings in the Theory of Economic Development.* London : Basil Blackwell.

Mookherjee, D and Ray (2002b). Is Equality Stable? *American Economic Review* **92**, 253-259.

Mookherjee, D and Ray (2003). Persistent Inequality. *Review of Economic Studies* **70**, 369-394.

Olive (2013). Daily Monitor (23rd April 2013). Kampala

Paulson, Anna and Robert Townsend (2004). Entrepreneurship and financial constraints in Thailand. *Journal of corporate finance* 10(2), 229-262.

Powell, Christine, Sally Grantham- McGregor, and M. Elston(1983). An evaluation of giving the Jamaican government meal to a class of children. *Human nutrition: Clinical nutrition* 37C, 381- 388

Psacharopoulos, George (1973). *Returns to Education. An International comparison.* San Francisco: Jossy Bass- Elsevior.

Psachapoulos (1985). Returns to Education. A further international update and implications. *Journal of Human Resources* 20(4): 583-604)

Psachapoulos (1994). Returns to Investiment in Education. : *A global update World Development* 22(9): 1325-1343.

Quadrini, Vincenco (1999). The Importance of Entreprenuership for wealth concentration and mobility. *Review of income and wealth* 45, 1-19.

Psachapoulos (2002). Returns to Investment in Education. *A global update World Development* 22(9):1325- 1343

Ray, D.(1998). *Development Economics*. Princeton, NJ: Princeton University Press.

Ricardo, D.(1951). *On the Principles of Political Economy and Taxation,* 1st ed. 1817, 3rd ed, 1821. In Vol of *the Works and Coreespondence of David Ricardo*. Cambridge:Cambridge University Press.

Romer, P(1986). Increasing Returns and Long-Run Growth. *Journal of Political Economy* **92**, 1002-1037.

Sen, A. (1999). *Development as Freedom*. New York: Alfred A. Knopf.

Schachtar, S., and Singer, J.(1962). Cognitive, Social and Physiological determinants of emotional state. Physiological Review 69: 379-399.

Skiba, A.K (1978). Optimal growth with a convex- concave production function. *Econometrica* 46, 527-539.

Solow, R.M.(1956). 'A Contribution to the Theory of Economic Growth' *Quarterly Journal of Economics*, **70**, 65-94.

Strauss John and Duncan Thomas (1995). Human Resources: Emperical modeling of household and family decisions. In Handbook of Development Economics, ed Jere Behrman and T.N Srinivansan Vol 3A (Amsterdam: North Holland) Chap 34 ppm1885-2023

Strauss John and Duncan Thomas (1998). Health, nutrition and economic development. *Journal of economic literature* 36(2) 766-817

Sunday vision (16th June 2013). Kampala: Uganda.

Svensson, Jakob (1998). Investment, Property rights and Political Instability. Theory and evidence. *European Economic Review* 42(7) 1317-1341

Thomas, Duncan (2001). Health, nutrition and economic prosperity. A macro economic perspective. Working paper, bulletin of the world working paper 7, working group 1, WHO commission macroeconomics and Health.

Torrens,R.(1820). *An Essay on the Influence of the External Corn Trade upon the production and Distribution of National Wealth*, 2nd ed. London: Hatchard.

Torrens, R.(1821). *An Essay on the Production of Wealth*. London: Longman, Hurst, Rees.

Usher, D.(1978). *An Imputation to the measure of Economic Growth for changes in life expectancy*. New York : National Bureau of Economic Research.

Zolt B., and Ping W. (1997). Financial development and growth. *Journal of Economic Review*, Federal Reserve Bank of Atlanta.

http://www.studymode.com/essays/Fei-Ranis-Theory-465461.html

www.ingramcontent.com/pod-product-compliance
Lightning Source LLC
La Vergne TN
LVHW102228300926
849160LV00005B/70
* 9 7 8 3 9 5 4 8 9 1 6 4 1 *